PERFORMANCE
EDITIONS

MOZART
SIX VIENNESE SONATINAS

Edited and Recorded by Christopher Harding

On the cover:
The Belvedere from Gesehen, Vienna
by Bernardo Bellotto
(1720–1780)
© Kunsthistorisches Museum, Vienna, Austria
The Bridgeman Art Library

ISBN 978-1-4234-8305-2

G. SCHIRMER, *Inc.*

DISTRIBUTED BY

HAL•LEONARD®
7777 W. BLUEMOUND RD. P.O. BOX 13819 MILWAUKEE, WI 53213

www.musicsalesclassical.com
www.halleonard.com

CONTENTS

The price of this publication includes access to companion recorded performances online, for download or streaming, using the unique code found on the title page.
Visit www.halleonard.com/mylibrary and enter the access code.

HISTORICAL NOTES

Wolfgang Amadeus Mozart (1756–1791)

Johann Chrysostom Wolfgang Amadeus Mozart was the seventh child of Leopold and Maria Anna Mozart, the second of only two of their children to survive. His sister, named for their mother and affectionately known in the family as 'Nannerl,' was a little more than four years older and significantly talented in her own right, if not equal to her brother, who must be regarded as one of the most astonishing musical prodigies of all time. The two children were lovingly and diligently educated by their father, in a curriculum that included mathematics, languages, literature, dancing, religious instruction, and, of course, all aspects of musical composition and performance. His greatness as a teacher to his children can be measured by their lasting accomplishments and international fame: all Europe seemed astonished by their performances at the keyboard, and Wolfgang's playing of the violin. And the boy impressed still more as a composer, having produced his first compositions by the age of five, and demonstrating an admirable ability to improvise with sophistication and passion.

Leopold undertook several tours of Europe with his children, lasting at times for several years. These trips to England, France, Italy and many parts of Germany and Austria served to further the fortunes and renown of the Mozart family, but also as critical educational experiences for Wolfgang and Nannerl. They met the most important and active musicians of the day, and performed for many important patrons of the arts among the nobility and political elite. This latter aspect of their travels was an essential part of an important long-range goal in the mind of Leopold: the procurement of a musical post worthy of the talents of his son. For many reasons beyond his control and despite his unflagging efforts, Leopold never realized this ambition, and lived only long enough to see his son struggle with the vicissitudes of life as a freelance composer and performer in the Vienna of the 1780s.

Wolfgang had been employed as an organist and composer of church music at various times by the Archbishop Colloredo of Salzburg, who also employed his father, and in which town Wolfgang was born and raised. Wolfgang appears to have been exceedingly unhappy with both his duties and his treatment as a servant in the Archbishop's retinue; however, things came to a head with the Archbishop in 1781, with Wolfgang dismissed with a literal kick in the rear. This inauspicious event led to a decade of struggle as an independent musician in the Austrian capital Vienna, and fortunately for us, led Mozart to produce a priceless body of music in all genres: solo and concerto works for piano, operas, chamber music, symphonies; the list goes on and on.

Mozart received a great deal of public adulation and support during his years in Vienna—for a time. Without a reliable and steady income from some court-appointed post, the best way to support himself and his family (he married Constanze Weber 1782; the couple had six children, only two of whom survived infancy) was to teach privately, organize performances of new works and to publish compositions. These latter activities, as remains the case today, were highly uncertain as sources of income, and although Mozart was extraordinarily industrious and active, the young family was in constant financial peril despite many public triumphs. Towards the end of his life, Mozart did receive a small salary as a court chamber musician, but public performances had all but dried up for him, and returns from the sale of his compositions were highly variable. Mozart turned for help to many patrons and friends, including the members of the Viennese Freemasons.

Mozart joined the Freemasons in 1784, a society that included many musicians and patrons of the arts, nobility and commoners alike. Mozart's father and Joseph Haydn also became members. The ideology behind this movement was concerned in part with the ennobling of one's spirit and character through self-knowledge and the brotherhood of like-minded members; some of these ideas find expression in certain elements of Mozart's music, most notably in his penultimate opera, *Die Zauberflöte* ("The Magic Flute").

Despite the help of his friends and success from several important commissions, Mozart's last year was marked by financial anxiety and serious illness. He worked to his last hours on a Requiem mass commissioned by Count Walsegg-Stuppach, under conditions of secrecy; the work was finished by Mozart's associate Franz Xaver Süssmayr in order to fulfill the commission, a very material help to Constanze and her children. This, with subsequent benefit concerts and the publication of many of Mozart's unpublished works, enabled the family to pay off their debts and educate the children, one of whom (Franz Xaver) became an accomplished musician in his own right. These publications also preserved for us a body of work that today is regarded as one of the most sublime and greatest achievements of western music.

PERFORMANCE NOTES

Notes on the Edition

This performance edition of the Six Viennese Sonatinas for piano is based on a fine 1959 edition by Joseph Prostakoff, published by G. Schirmer. The pieces that comprise the individual movements of the sonatinas were originally composed for a trio of basset horns, an instrument that sounds as the baritone member of the clarinet family. Mozart knew many clarinet and basset horn players during his Vienna years; several were fellow Masons, and Mozart wrote much music to be played by them at lodge meetings. These particular pieces were written as serenade music, to be performed as background music to a dinner or some other social function, or else to be played purely for pleasure in some private venue. They were never published in any form during Mozart's lifetime, and the autograph has been lost.

Shortly after Mozart's death, the twenty-five pieces in the original collection were arranged into five multi-movement Divertimenti, known today as K. 439b. Several versions were published for various instrumental combinations as well as for solo piano, to capitalize on the growing market for music for amateurs. The solo piano arrangement, however, freely re-orders the movements of the original set into six sonatinas, and in at least two cases creates a new combination of menuet and trio from what are in reality completely different movements. According to Prostakoff, the quality of the original transcription "is very uneven," when compared to the original instrumental version. He successfully and intelligently addresses these deficiencies in his own transcription of the originals, restoring cut sections to fully round out the form of several movements, and restoring harmonic textures and melodic shapes to more closely follow Mozart's original intentions.

In this edition, I have again compared Prostakoff's edition with the original instrumental version as published in the *Neue Mozart-Ausgabe* by Bärenreiter-Verlag. My concern has been to remove or clearly distinguish Prostakoff's interpretations and additions to the text wherever they seemed to distort the grace and charm of Mozart's original intentions and playful inventiveness. Prostakoff's ideas are often quite fine, but Mozart's indications have the advantage of being clear while also allowing for personal creativity, especially in dynamic issues. I have also restored some of Mozart's original notation to conform to what students today will encounter in Mozart's more advanced piano works, principally in matters of trills (which always start on the note above the principal note, except when the upper trill note immediately precedes the trill) and appoggiaturas (always played on the downbeat, as realized in the score). I have ventured to offer fingering suggestions more in line with classic piano technique as well.

The essence of Mozart's music is a profound elegance of an intensely beautiful and singing eloquence. Despite their humble purposes of soothing entertainment (in the mind of Mozart) and the instruction of advanced intermediate students (the use to which we often put them today), these sonatinas bear the unmistakable stamp of their composer. His genius turned practically everything he touched to purest gold, and that is exactly what we can find in these works if we approach them with the expectation of finding joy, which turns out to be the whole reason for their existence.

Notes on Performing the Piano Music of Mozart

Mozart's music captures an elegance and beauty that has all but faded from modern society and culture. This loss is one of the reasons that it is so vitally important to cherish and promote the study and performance of his work. In exploring for ourselves or with our students, we open the door to a life changing experience, at least in musical terms. All great music has something to teach us about the truth of human experience for those with ears to hear and understand it.

When studying the piano music of Mozart, we must be sure to address several musical issues that are crucial to producing a performance that captures the essence of Mozart's style and personality. Chief among these issues are precise articulation and phrasing, a discreet (but liberal) use of the damper pedal, voicing on the modern piano, and above all, an elegance of meter and a singing sound.

Mozart was trained as a harpsichordist in his youth, and his growth into adulthood coincided with the explosion in popularity and rapid mechanical improvement of the fortepiano, which displaced the harpsichord as the instrument of choice both for composers and the general public by the middle 1770s. One difference between the instrument that Mozart knew and our modern instrument is the notion that the former is a "speaking" instrument, while our concern these days is how to make our instrument "sing." In fact, Mozart's music is very vocal in character. It is possible to speak with eloquence and vivacity, and to sing with beautiful sound on both the fortepiano of his day and on our own instrument.

Articulation and Phrasing

Mozart tends to employ very short slurs that often encompass as little as two notes and almost never cross the bar line. He presumes that the performer will understand how to sculpt a long line out of his musical gestures, an assumption not shared by later editors of his work who blithely changed the original slur markings to dictate the length and shape of complete musical phrases. In so doing, they lose both the freedom that Mozart bequeaths to his performers in matters of musical inflection, and obscure his clues as to sculpting the smaller musical gestures that make up each phrase. Mozart's slurs show us the individual words in each musical sentence, as it were. How we pronounce each word greatly impacts the character of the music and produces its "speaking" quality. The length and shape of each sentence, however, is left to our own discretion as thinking and feeling musicians.

A slur, as used in classic notation, indicates that the first note of each gesture so marked is to be played as the loudest note, the impetus of the group. What follows is a tiny, legato decrescendo to the last note of the group, which is the softest and shortest in articulation, even if all notes of the group have the same value. A string of eighth notes, for example:

One of the reasons for finishing a slur soft and short is to make sure that the following note is articulated well. Very often pianists lift the hand to provide a non-legato "space" before the next slur or note. This is a matter of proper musical "pronunciation" as well as phrase inflection. In fact, it is also the source of great interpretive freedom: it is true that the second note in a two-note slur (for example) is always softer and shorter than the first note, even if they have the same rhythmic value. But *how much* shorter, or *how much* softer, is an individual choice that profoundly affects the character of each slur.

It is not always the case that one has to provide a physical or aural space at the end of each slur. For example, when Mozart employs measure-long slurs over successive measures:

In such instances, we should feel free to play in a legato manner, without lifting at the end of each slur. It is also possible to use the pedal on the modern piano in such a way as to capture both the articulated release of each gesture and a continuous, singing sound; I discuss this possibility below in the section on Pedaling. In this way a performance that sounds too exaggerated or clipped in its articulation can be avoided, and the flowing quality ("like oil") that Mozart advocates in several of his letters is achieved.

All staccato markings in this edition are Mozart's unless discussed in the notes to each movement; I have retained some of Prostakoff's staccato markings and added a few of my own when the character of the movement encourages this. Mozart also employs a *portato* marking

which indicates to play the notes with a slightly longer articulation than a normal staccato.

Technique and Fingering

Just as the two-note slur forms the basic unit of classic musical gestures, it also forms the basic physical motion of modern piano technique. In properly executing a two-note slur, allow the hand (and consequently the finger, which accepts the weight of arm) to drop into the first note by means of the wrist, which rebounds to help the finger (hand) to rise out of the next key, the next note of the slur. In this way, we get two-notes out of one "double drop" motion, getting the second note "for free." This technique can be extended to address all the notes under a given slur, so that in a way, slurs can be understood to indicate technical gestures as well as musical ones. In fact, this is the secret to playing fast, easily: we arrange to play as many notes in one physical gesture as is possible and musically practical.

One of the most important and overlooked aspects of the "double drop" gesture, however, is the release of the gesture. This release by the hand, involving an upward rebound of the wrist, is crucial for preparing the articulation of the next physical and musical gesture. It also is the means by which the hand and arm travel to the next note, especially if that involves a change of hand position. In an exaggerated way, one can imagine the performance of a piece to be like a child bouncing from trampoline to trampoline, as the hand travels by means of a rebounding wrist from hand position to hand position throughout the piece. Be careful not to exaggerate this motion, however, lest our technique and performance become awkward and overly vertical—Mozart himself criticized this type of playing very severely.

By using this controlled bouncing technique to articulate slurs and detached notes, we can arrive at a freedom in our fingering choices that allows us great comfort and efficient motion within hand positions. We can also achieve an easier legato, especially in passages involving double thirds or finger crossings. It is with this in mind that I have notated fingering suggestions. Different hands will undoubtedly prefer different fingerings.

Voicing

One of the great differences between the fortepiano of Mozart's day and our modern instrument is the increased resonance and thick textures produced by the bass strings of the latter. As pianos became stronger and heavier in construction and needed to project in larger spaces, the light and comparatively transparent sound of the fortepiano was lost in the quest for greater resonance and a more singing sound. Be careful on our modern instruments not to swamp the melodic clarity so vital to classic piano music with thick accompaniment textures—and be careful to preserve the rhythmic vitality and "melodic" shapes of those accompaniments.

It is not enough to say simply that accompaniments must be softer than melodies. Chords and Alberti bass figures should be voiced so that the individual notes sound with a naturally clear balance. In chords and octaves, this often means adding weight to the upper notes of the chord (and subtracting weight from the lower notes), to a greater or lesser degree depending on the register of the piano.

Alberti bass figures, whether of the slow and melodic type or the fast and rhythmic type, must be understood in terms of the function of each note in the pattern. The bass note is always the most important, sounding the loudest in comparison to the others. In slow, melodic Aberti basses, the bass note can be held to produce a finger pedal, thus taking advantage of the resonance of the modern piano (although Mozart often employed this technique on the fortepiano as well). The third note in the pattern is next in aural importance, with the repeated second and fourth notes being least important and least weighted.

An excellent way to practice Alberti bass patterns is to hold the thumb down completely while bouncing with the hand from the bass note to the third note of the pattern. A double drop will often serve to get these two notes out of one physical gesture; once this is mastered, allow the thumb to play its notes normally, as part of the hand's double drop gesture. This technique can attune the ear to hearing the function and balance of the individual notes in the pattern, as well as teaching the hand to get as many notes as possible "for free."

A further note about playing legato thirds and sixths in one hand: if we can play one voice legato with our fingers and wrist motion (usually the top voice), then the other voice may be played non-legato while gliding along in as smooth a manner as possible. The effect is legato in sound, if not in fact. In any case, whenever we encounter thirds and sixths in Mozart, we generally voice the top note. A good way to practice for this is to use two hands first to play the thirds or sixths with the proper sound, and then to use one hand. After this, one might try playing the thirds or sixths with one hand, but playing the top note legato and the bottom note staccato. Another very useful strategy is to play the top voice alone with the fingering used when playing both together, and then the bottom voice with its own fingering, and then to put the voices back together.

Pedaling

Along with voicing, a great deal of attention must be paid to how we use the damper pedal in Mozart's music. (The *una corda* certainly can be used for color, but will not be discussed here.) It is important to remember that we can and should use a lot of pedal in playing this music, but also that we should strive to make it "invisible." As a general rule, if the audience hears our pedal, it is too much for Mozart.

I have a personal rule for pedaling Mozart's music: no more than two consecutive notes in a single pedal. I break this rule all the time, especially if I am pedaling for the sake of extending a harmony, or to add a glossy sheen of brilliance to an extended scale passage over a single harmony. Use of the pedal is ideal for helping to warm up the legato of two-note slurs. The most useful pedaling on our modern instrument is what we call syncopated pedal: depressing the pedal after playing a certain note or chord, and lifting it as we play the next note chord, only to depress it again afterwards.

Such pedaling effectively hides itself inside the sound of the notes and chords, adding a sense of warmth and resonance somewhat akin to the vibrato of string instruments. If used tastefully, it can also conceal the often jarring hiccup we can experience upon releasing the key at the end of slurs. Pedaling in no way relieves fingers of the task of clearly articulating the notes and ends of slurs, or of producing true legato; fingers must work very conscientiously to speak through the effects produced by using the pedals. For this reason, I suggest a lot of practice without the pedal to hear exactly what our fingers are doing, and to develop a sense of where the pedal is essential and where it is *not*.

I have chosen not to notate pedalings in the present edition, following Prostakoff's (and indeed Mozart's) own example. The reason is that it is practically impossible to notate with acceptable precision something that changes from piano to piano, room to room, and performer to performer. Pedaling is one of the most personal aspects of playing the piano, and can be developed and refined only with much experimentation and guidance from our own ears and those of our teachers who are actually in the same room. Intentional listening, combined with a clear sense of pure and beautiful sound, is the key.

Dynamics and Tempos

Mozart uses dynamic indications sparsely, and limits them to blocks of music marked to be played *"forte"* or *"piano"* with very little direction for nuance. We can infer, however, from certain movements where (for example) a *forte* section is followed by another *forte* section with no intervening soft indication, that Mozart presumes that the performer will express dynamic inflections and nuances within the *forte* character. Moderate *crescendos* and *decrescendos* serve to highlight the shape of certain musical lines, and the suggestions left to us by Prostakoff (marked in brackets) serve as an excellent starting point to encourage our imagination and taste. A radical change of dynamic may also serve to increase the playfulness or variety of character within a certain section, especially in regard to phrases repeated verbatim. The articulations of bass line accompaniments might be treated with similar freedom, as different articulations produce different characters.

When determining a tempo, consideration must always be given to the meter of a movement. The hierarchy of beats to be found in any given measure must be well understood, in order to avoid two common faults: first, the fault of playing each pulse equally (instead of a strong downbeat, weaker subsequent beats and an upbeat feeling before the next downbeat, etc.); second, the fault of changing the meter to encompass many more pulses than are actually written (counting in eighth notes when quarters are marked as the unit of pulse, for example). Both faults work against the flowing elegance Mozart calls for in his letters about performance practice. The Italian terms (*Allegro, Allegretto,* etc.) must of course be considered first, and with the understanding that they often indicate character as well as tempo. These must interact with our understanding of the meter to arrive at a proper performance tempo. Added to these must be the acoustics of the hall, the quality of a particular instrument's resonance, etc. From this we can see that the idea of tempo is not a starting point, but rather the end result of many different considerations, variable according to circumstance. My indications are given with this in mind.

The feeling of an established and constantly flowing meter is a large part of the elegance that Mozart's music requires, much in the same way that a waltz requires a consistent flow and lilt. However, all classic music makes use of agogic placements, little hesitations, and unwritten rests that are employed for rhetorical effect between phrases, sections, or to emphasize something special. We can also choose to feel the number of beats per measure more strongly or more freely ("in one"), a useful technique when we wish to change the character of a piece but not its tempo. Make sure to establish some metrical consistency to achieve rhetorical and dramatic effects. An unyielding or inexorable meter becomes a tyrannous elegance, not the gracious eloquence of Mozart.

Repeats

Musicologists will tell us that every repeat is to be taken in sonata forms and variations, and that certainly would apply to the simple binary or rondo forms that predominate in these sonatina movements as well. There are solid dramatic and harmonic reasons behind this stance. Since the performance of these works was meant for private enjoyment, however, I see nothing wrong with encouraging ourselves to do as we please regarding the repeats!

Notes to the Sonatinas

SONATINA NO. 1 IN C MAJOR
Allegro (K.439b, No. 16)

m. 9: Try to slide the thumb for legato in the alto voice of the RH.

m. 11: The LH articulations are mine; also m. 55.

mm. 24–25: These *sf* markings are Mozart's!

m. 28: Be sure to end soft!

m. 33: The C in the alto voice of the RH is tied to the next measure; we must take care not to repeat it on the next downbeat. Also mm. 35 and 37.

m. 70 and following: Take care to shape a long horizontal line, avoiding choppy verticality.

Menuetto and Trio: Allegretto (K.439b, No. 7)

mm. 25–31: The LH articulations are mine. Also mm. 68–70.

Adagio (K.439b No. 23)

m. 1: It is important to feel this movement in 2, not in 4, according to the *alla breve* time signature. The turn should be executed in a vocal manner, with every note singing and important, but perhaps placed as late as possible.

m. 3: Take care to shape the staccato chords, to avoid an unmusical verticality.

m. 4: The LH should take care not to bump the D after the tied C, since Mozart slurs over this note.

Rondo: Allegretto (K.439b, No. 20)

m.1: There is also an alternate Allegro marking for this movement.

m. 14: Take great care to finish the phrase on the third eighth note, and begin the new phrase with the *subito forte* on the fourth eight note.

mm. 22–23: The LH articulations are Prostakoff's.

m. 23: We would start the RH trill on the A, the principal note, because the upper note (B-flat) immediately precedes the trill and it would be redundant to repeat the note. The same holds true for m. 31, start the RH trill on the D.

mm. 25–26: Be careful about the voicing of the RH, in order to distinguish the two different lines; also in mm. 89–90.

m. 52: The *fp* is Mozart's! The repeated phrases here and from mm. 57–64 offer opportunities for dynamic variation.

mm. 94–99: The LH articulations are Prostakoff's.

SONATINA NO. 2 IN A MAJOR
Allegro (K.439b, No. 6)

m. 1 and similar: The grace notes are not Mozart's, but form a stylish flourish to begin the piece.

mm. 9–11: The RH needs to make use of a double drop from the wrist for each of these musical and technical gestures. (See the section entitled "Technique and Fingering" beginning on page 7 for an explanation of the double drop technique.)

mm. 20–21: The finger substitution in the alto voice is tricky; hold the thumb in place until after the soprano has accomplished its finger substitution, at which point switch to the second finger in the alto.

m. 36: I prefer Prostakoff's ossia.

Menuetto (from K.439b, No. 4) and Trio (from K.439b, No. 2): Allegretto

mm. 6–8: Prostakoff had added staccato markings to the single quarter notes, but I don't feel that these need to be as short as that articulation would imply.

mm. 16–17: A very rare instance of Mozart himself extending the slur over the barline.

Adagio (K.439b, No. 21)

m. 16: Be sure to release the third finger before throwing to the thumb in the RH on the second beat.

m. 17: In this measure, throw the RH from the first to the second beats.

m. 21: The alto voice, from beat three on, as legato as possible until the downbeat of m. 22.

Rondo: Allegro (K.439b No. 10)

m. 43: Using the fourth finger for the repeated notes of the LH helps produce a better hand staccato.

m. 47: Be sure to drop from the wrist on the downbeat to get all the RH sixths in one physical gesture.

mm.101–104: You don't have to hold the LH quarter notes for their full value; a little tenuto nudge is all that is required to mark the bass.

m. 122: In classic music, a *fermata* is a signal for a small cadenza (cadence), or lead-in to the next phrase. I would encourage a short arpeggiation or scale that decorates the harmony here.

mm. 147–154: The incredibly long slur over the RH voices is Mozart's!

SONATINA NO. 3 IN D MAJOR
Adagio (K.439b, No. 3)

m.5: The triplets in the ossia can be best negotiated by a drop from the wrist, followed by a roll out of the last third. The thumb should be very relaxed and should travel with the hand.

m. 8: The *sf* is Mozart's!

m. 11: A touch of pedal increases the beauty of the LH diads, which are Mozart's.

Menuetto and Trio: Allegretto (K.439b, No. 22)

m. 23: This trill starts on the upper note, B. Release the thumb on the C-sharp as soon as you like, to change fingers on the trill.

m. 39 and similar: It is very typical of Mozart to use finger pedal in his piano accompaniments.

Rondo: Allegro (K.439b, No. 5)

m. 4: The grace note is Prostakoff's solution for a trill in the original.

mm. 21–22: The RH alone should play the thirds of the first beat of m. 21; thereafter, until the down beat of m. 23, the LH should take the lower voice.

mm. 49–81: These repeated phrases offer perfect opportunities for dynamic variation. The *p* repeats are Mozart's.

SONATINA NO. 4 IN B-FLAT MAJOR
Romanze: Andante (K.439b, No. 24)

m. 1: Remember to feel this Andante in *alla breve* (cut) time.

mm. 9–11: The LH slurs and articulations are Prostakoff's. Also in mm. 13–15.

m. 27: The trill which sounds on the third beat is started on the D because Mozart notates this with a grace note. It is not absolutely necessary to hold the A in the alto voice as you execute the trill.

Menuetto (from K.439b, No. 18) and Trio (from K.439b, No. 4): Allegretto

m. 3 and similar: The slur in the alto voice of the RH is very challenging to play in combination with the staccato soprano. In fact, it is a perfect example of a method of practicing good voicing: staccato one voice, legato the other.

m. 15: Be careful to bring out the LH melody.

m. 24 and similar: The final note in the slurred triplet needs to be played staccato. The RH sixteenth note which appears as an upbeat to m. 25 should actually be played as a triplet, played with the last note of the LH. This follows an old convention of notation for coordinating triplet rhythms between the hands.

m. 25: The *fp* marking is Mozart's!

m. 37: The sixteenth note is treated as a triplet, matching the last note of the LH triplet on beat 1

Rondo: Allegro assai (K.439b, No. 15)

m. 1 and similar: Be sure to "collect" the LH when playing the repeated notes, to avoid keeping the hand stretched out over the octave unnecessarily.

m. 9 and similar: Be sure to accent the beginning of each slur in the LH and RH for a real dialogue between the voices.

m. 39: The grace note is Mozart's, and this is executed on the beat as a fast grace note, instead of as a sixteenth note.

mm. 50–52: The sixteenth note pickups should be accomplished with fast "double drops" of the wrist. (See the section entitled "Technique and Fingering" beginning on page 7 for an explanation of the double drop technique.)

mm. 55: Be careful to observe the tied C in the LH as you fold your second finger over the thumb.

m. 71: The trill starts on the D while the RH thumb takes the B-flat; we can release the thumb as soon as we like, however, do not hold it out until the next downbeat.

mm. 91–95: It is possible to be legato in the alto voice of the RH, releasing the top voice after each tied note. The LH articulations are Prostakoff's.

mm. 109–110: Be sure to release the end of the slur in the RH going into m. 110 so you can drop into the down beat with your fourth finger.

mm. 112–113: Keep the top voice legato.

mm. 148–153: The LH accompaniment is Prostakoff's invention. Although it does not capture the shape of Mozart's problematic musical gestures, it does retain his harmonies.

SONATINA NO. 5 IN F MAJOR
Larghetto (K. 439b, No. 17)

m. 1: Despite the slow tempo marking, remember to feel this movement with an *alla breve* (cut time) meter. My tempo indication is given in quarter notes for the sake of practicality. The *"dolce"* marking is Mozart's!

m. 9 and similar: It is beautiful to lightly pedal each portato eighth note.

mm. 11–12: Prostakoff's hairpin is lovely, but should be accomplished by the RH only.

m. 13 and similar: The staccato tenuto markings are Prostakoff's.

Menuetto and Trio: Allegretto (K.439b, No. 12)

mm. 1–4: Be sure to carefully choreograph the release of the slurs, since different parts of the hand have to hold and release at different times.

mm. 24–25: The RH should take the alto voice with the thumb. This creates a challenge for the RH to throw the second finger to the C on the second eighth of m. 27, but the ease of the preceding measures is worth the tradeoff.

m. 26: Be sure to throw the LH fourth finger to the E on the third beat.

m. 39: Start the turn right in time on the "and" of the third beat, throwing from the thumb to the second finger on the downbeat of m. 40.

m. 45 and similar: Although we re-articulate the LH downbeat after a release from the previous measure, be sensitive to the resolution of the harmony.

mm. 59–60: The *sf*'s are Mozart's.

m. 75: The RH thumb must glide very lightly while the top fingers play legato, being sure to throw with the hand from the third to fifth fingers on the third beat.

Polonaise (K. 439b, No. 25)

m. 8: Prostakoff's ossia is worth the effort. One has to be mentally ready for it before it comes, since the level of difficulty dramatically increases if we take this option.

m. 9: I find that using this finger substitution creates a playful rhythm in my hand that suits the musical gesture.

SONATINA NO. 6 IN C MAJOR
Allegro (K.439b, No. 11)

m. 1: The tempo is fast because of the *alla breve* (cut) time signature.

m. 4 and similar: Allow the thumb to bounce along with a legato 2-note slur accomplished by the top fingers.

m. 6: Although the RH fingering on beat two is good for legato purposes, the wrist should still be used to negotiate the awkward stretch for the third finger.

m. 9: A slight release at the end of each RH slur is most correct

mm. 14–17: The LH should be sure to answer the RH with confidence

mm. 20–21: The LH slurs and staccato markings are Prostakoff's

mm. 23–24: Be sure to release the RH, but not the LH, which is slurred over the barline. Prostakoff's ossia is only if the thirds prove impossible to perform with grace.

mm. 33 and 34: Be sure to listen for the end of the phrase on the third eighth note before beginning the next phrase with the staccato "A" in the RH; mm. 90 and 92 pose similar challenges.

m. 94: Finish softly!

Menuetto (from K.439b, No. 2) and Trio (from K. 439b, No. 9): Allegretto

mm. 35–36: By voicing the top voice of the RH thirds and playing them with legato fingering, you can cover the fact that your thumb is not legato. The same is true for the RH of m. 44.

mm. 52–56: Make the voicing of the alto imitation very clear

m. 62: The thumb throws to the second beat in the RH; the same applies for the alto voice in m. 67.

Adagio (K.439b, No. 19)

m. 1: The "dolce" marking is Mozart's!

m. 9: It is beautiful to pedal each of the portato quarter notes.

mm. 13–14: Be extremely careful to differentiate the voices and not to poke the sixteenth notes! Sing through the sound of the long notes.

m. 15: The *mf* dynamic is mine, to indicate how far we should take Prostakoff's crescendo in m. 13.

mm. 15–16: Prostakoff has added a lower voice to the RH for pianistic and textural purposes. I would recommend no pedal for the staccato chords in m. 15.

Finale: Allegro (K. 439b, No. 1)

m. 1 and m. 72: Voicing the LH might be more interesting than bringing out the RH in this case.

m. 22: Be careful not to bang the second beat in either hand!

mm. 28–37: The release of the slurs in the RH require a great deal of choreography to execute well, with the top and bottom parts of the hand doing different things. This is excellent training for the Fugues of the *Well- Tempered Clavier*.

m. 34 and m. 95: Be sure to bring out the LH melody. The RH, although providing the accompaniment, must also be well voiced.

mm. 41 and 44, 110 and 113: the *sf*'s are Prostakoff's correct interpretation of Mozart's *forte* markings here.

m. 46: It may be useful to practice the RH thirds *molto staccatissimo* in order to get used to playing them with the hand and wrist, rather than the fingers.

m. 53: I prefer to hear a surprising accent on the second beat, to emphasize the dramatic G-sharp. But in the LH and RH of mm. 55–56 and similar, I would be careful to throw away the second beat rather than to emphasize it as in m. 53.

m. 119: I start the trill on the B, instead of the C as seems to be called for by the rule. My reason is that I want to hear a strong B on the downbeat of m. 119, which then resolves to the C on the downbeat of m. 120. Actually, in this piano rendition, the C sounds from the alto voice of m. 118, creating the illusion that the upper note of the trill immediately precedes the trill, in which case we would normally start on the principal note anyway.

Bibliography

Rosenblum, Sandra. *Performance Practices in Classic Piano Music*. Bloomington: Indiana University Press, 1988.

Recording Credits

Steinway Piano
David Lau, Recording Engineer
Hye-won Jung, Producer

SIX VIENNESE SONATINAS

Sonatina No. 1 in C Major

Wolfgang Amadeus Mozart

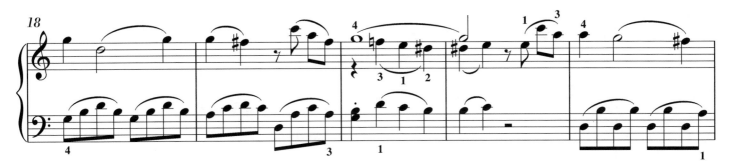

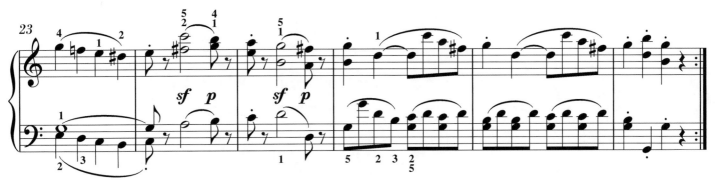

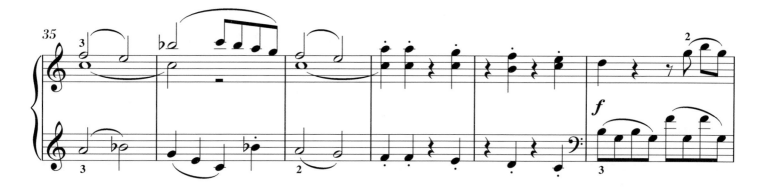

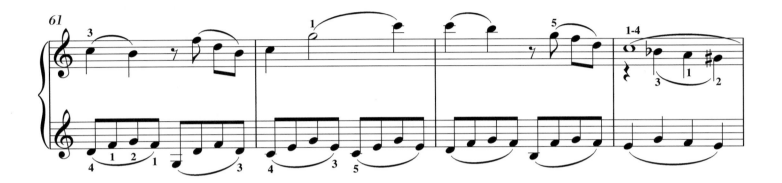

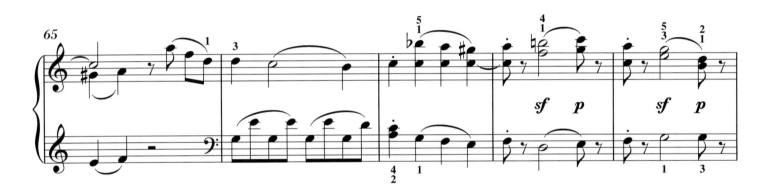

18

MENUETTO
Allegretto [♩ = 138]

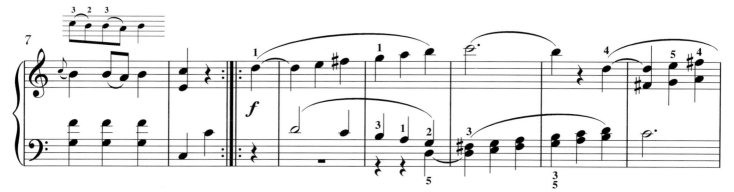

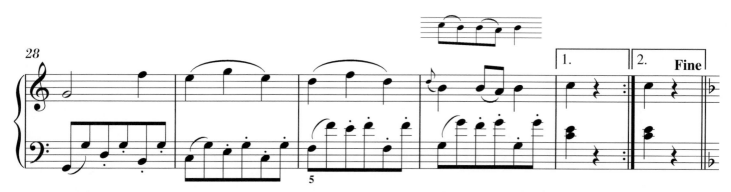

TRIO

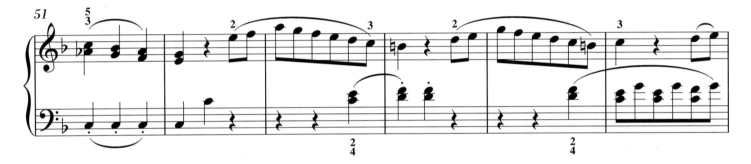

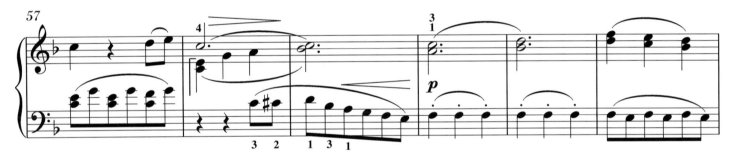

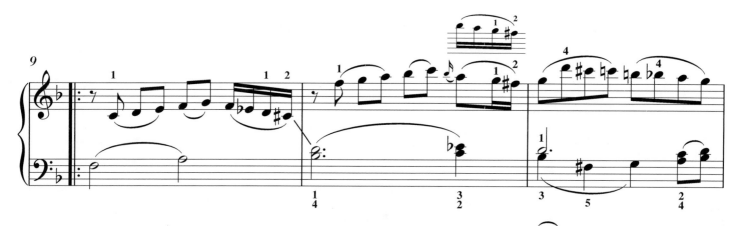

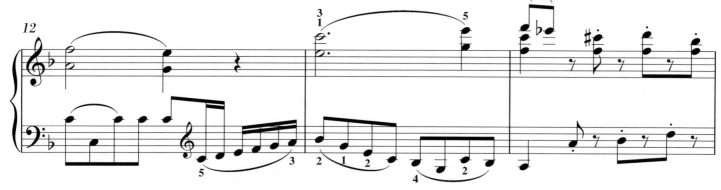

RONDO

Allegretto [♩ = 132]

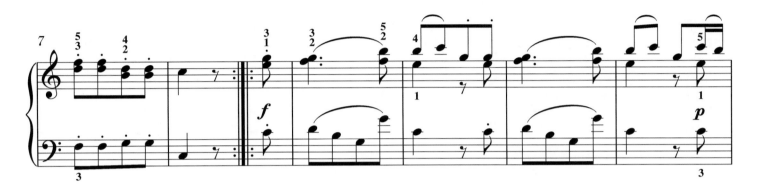

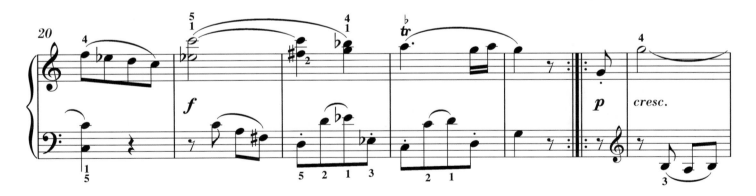

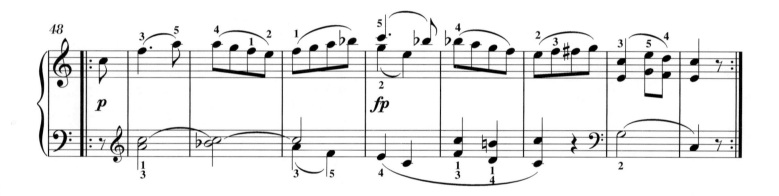

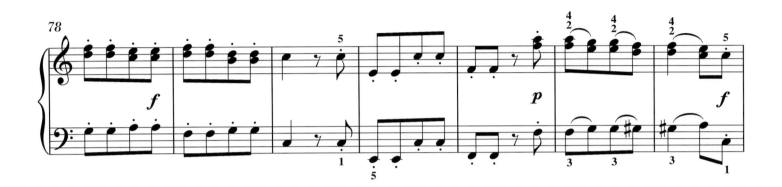

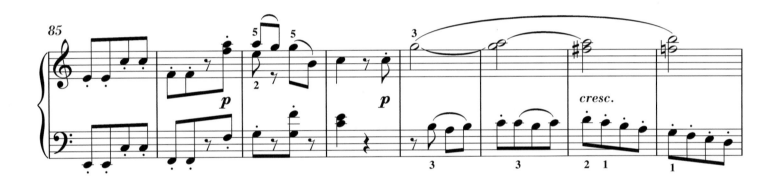

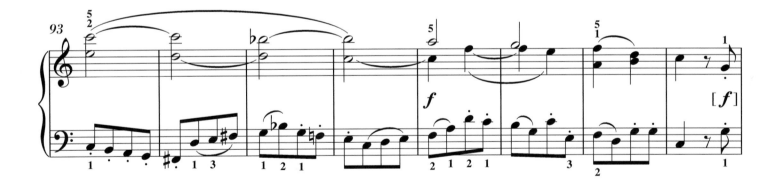

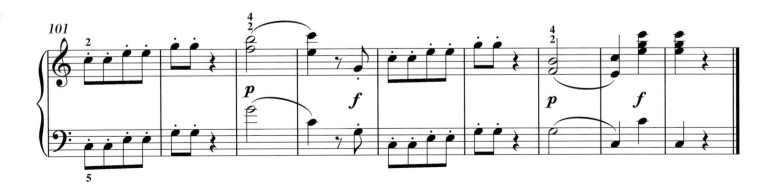

Sonatina No. 2 in A Major

Wolfgang Amadeus Mozart

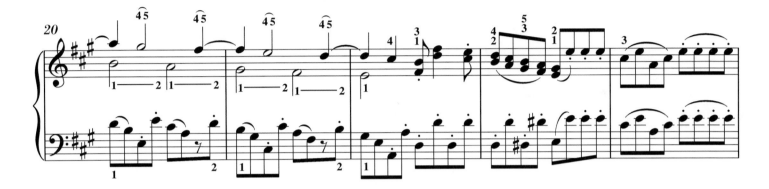

MENUETTO

Allegretto [♩ = 132]

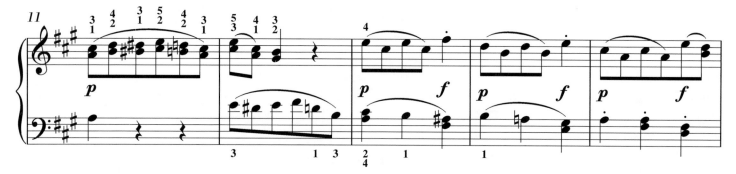

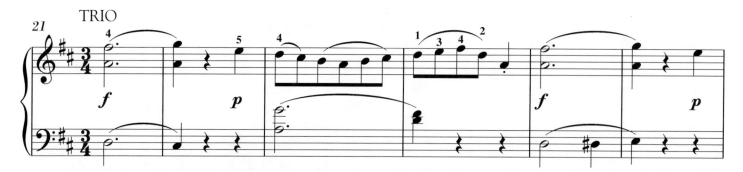

TRIO

*ossia

Adagio [♩ = 66]

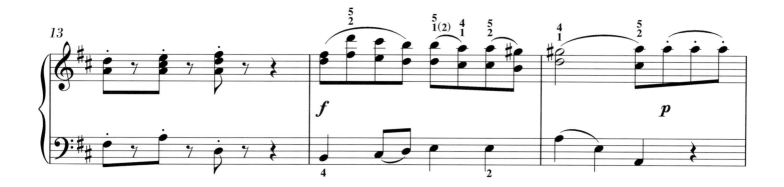

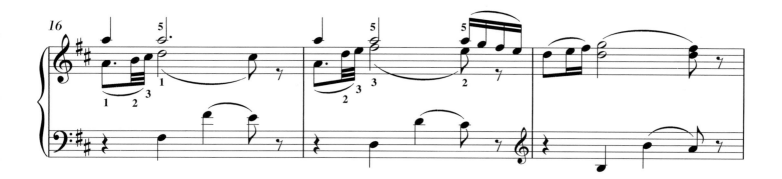

RONDO

Allegro [♩ = 138]

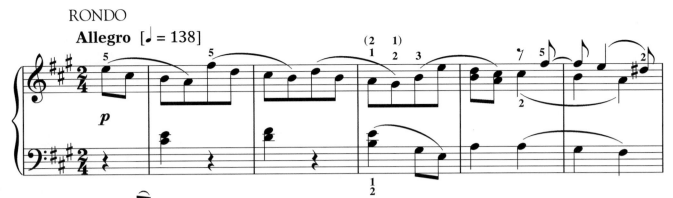

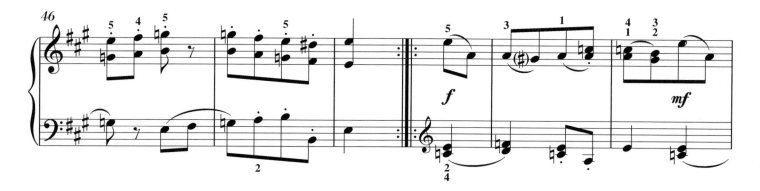

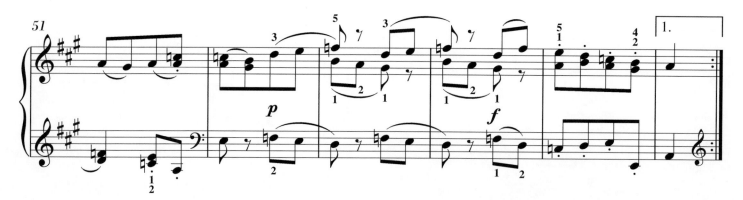

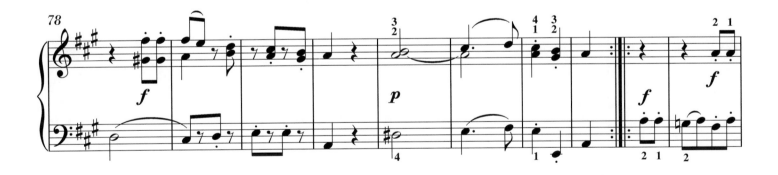

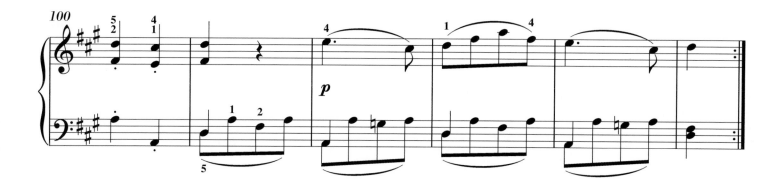

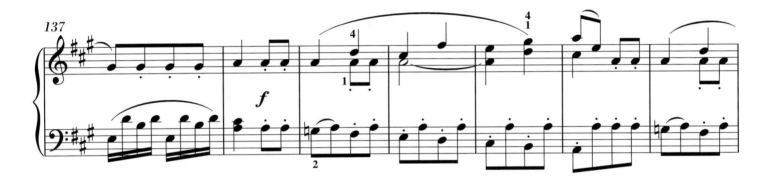

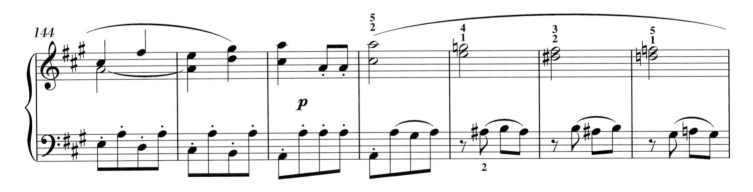

Sonatina No. 3 in D Major

Wolfgang Amadeus Mozart

MENUETTO

Allegretto [♩. = 50]

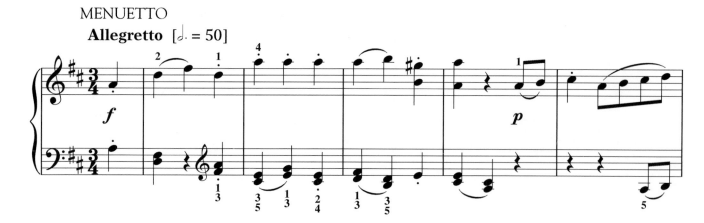

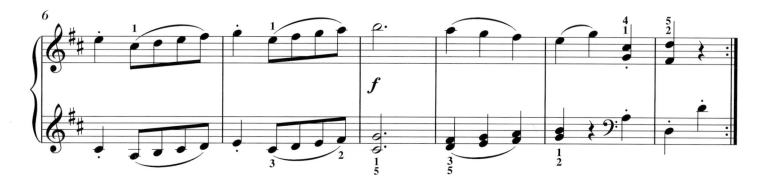

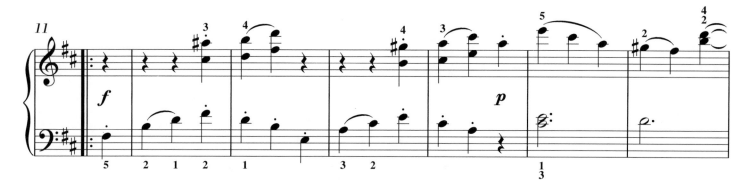

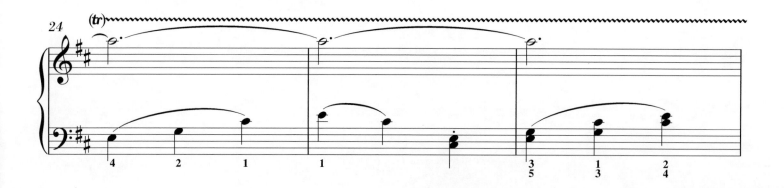

TRIO

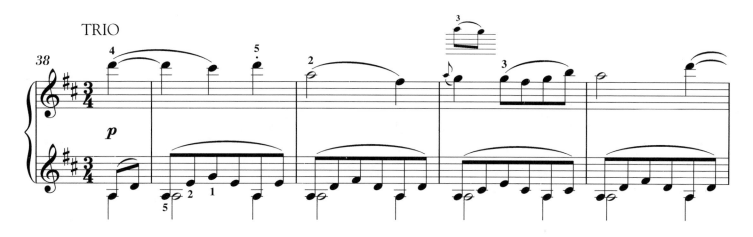

*Menuetto
da capo*

RONDO

Allegro [♩ = 138]

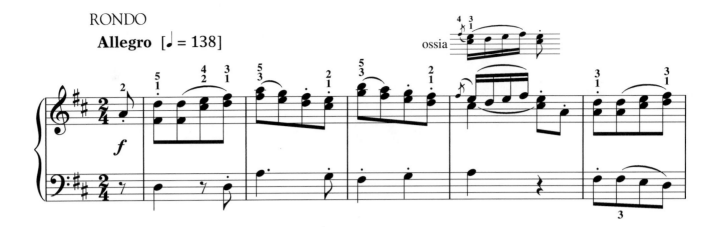

*ossia

ossia

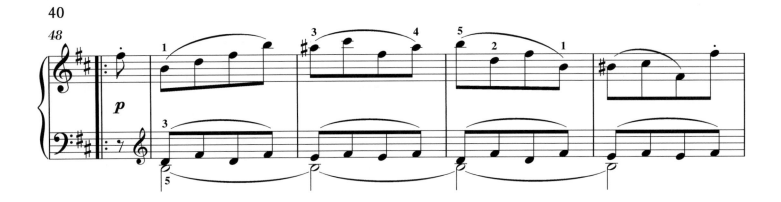

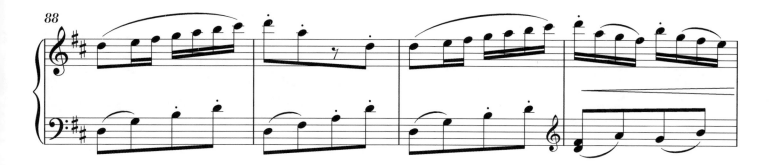

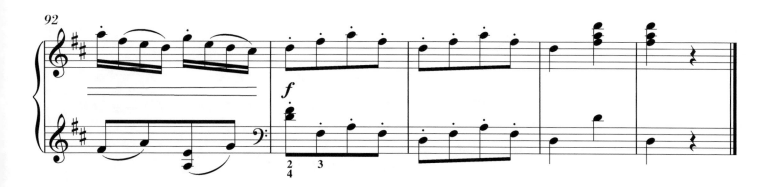

Sonatina No. 4 in B-flat Major

Wolfgang Amadeus Mozart

ROMANZE

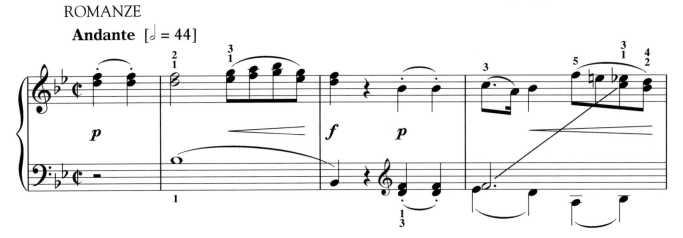

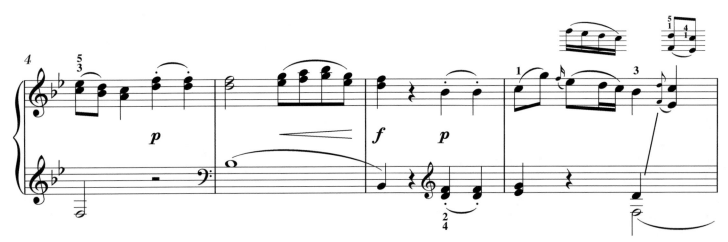

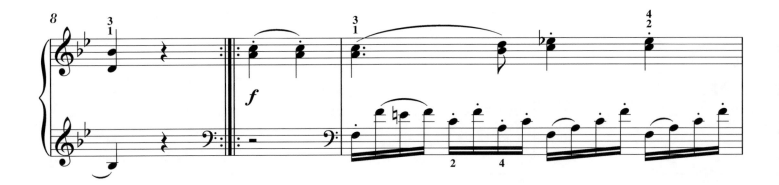

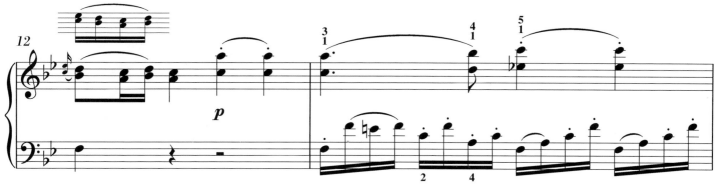

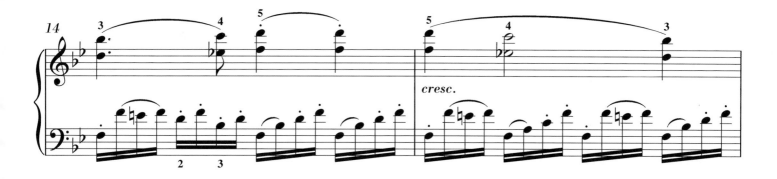

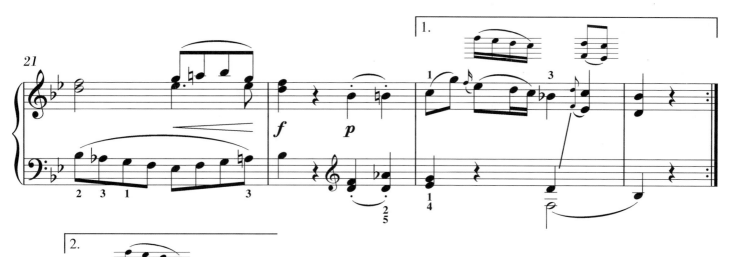

MENUETTO
Allegretto [♩ = 132]

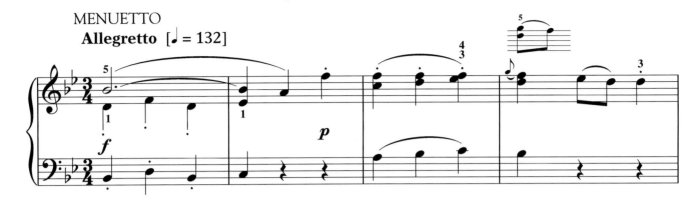

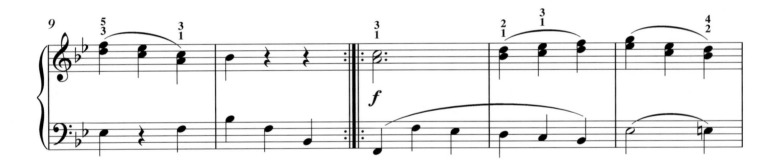

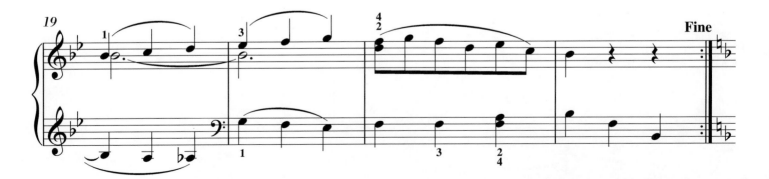

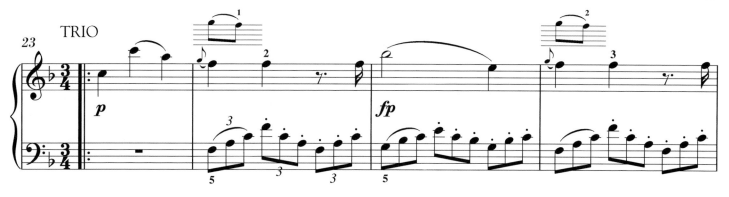

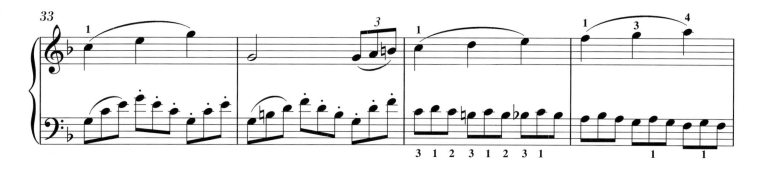

46

RONDO
Allegro assai [♩ = 138]

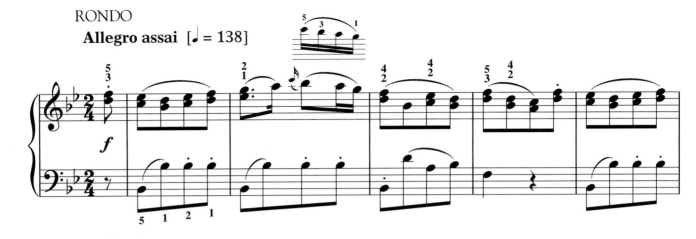

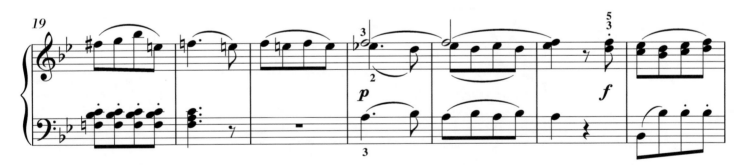

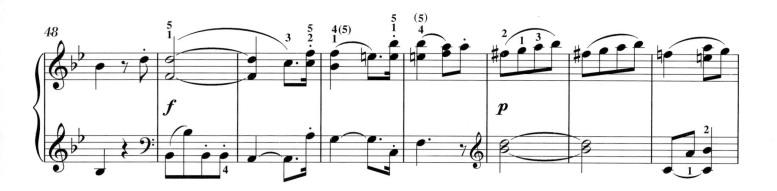

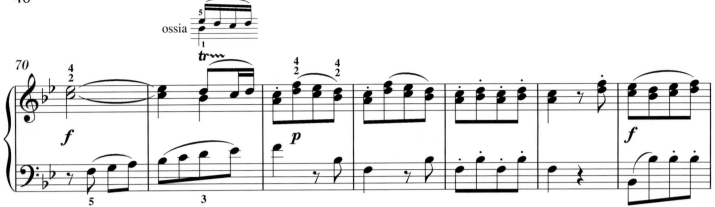

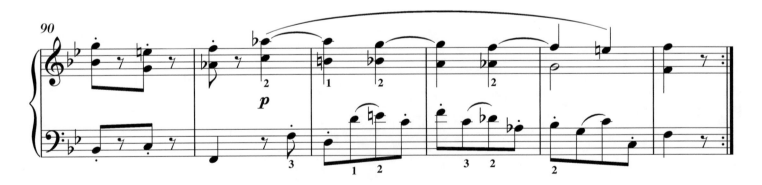

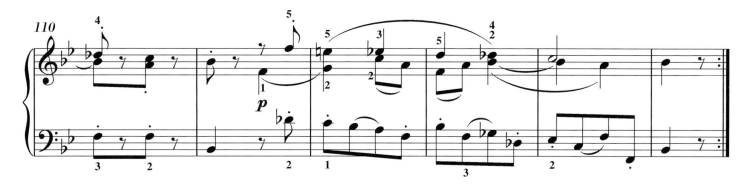

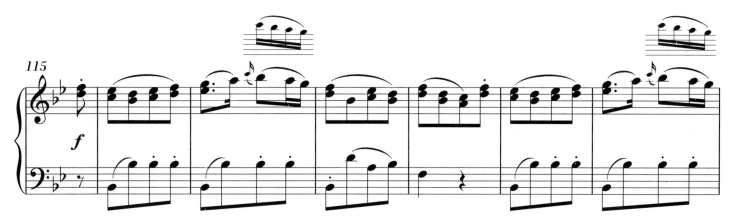

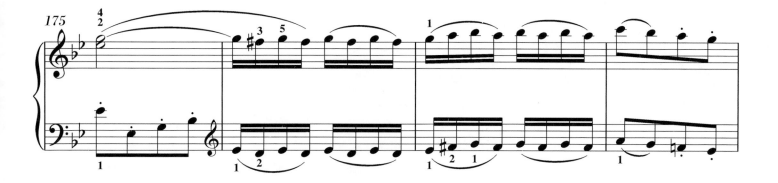

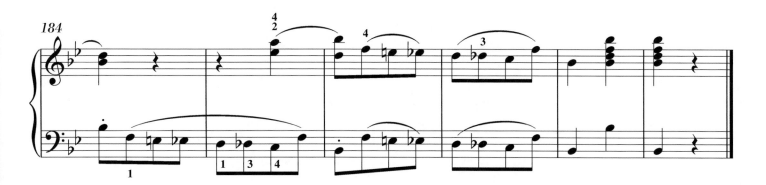

Sonatina No. 5 in F Major

Wolfgang Amadeus Mozart

Larghetto [♩ = 72]

MENUETTO

Allegretto [♩ = 126]

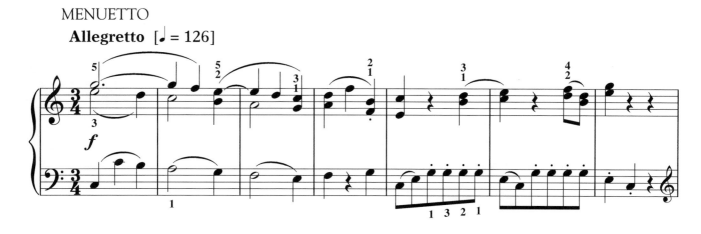

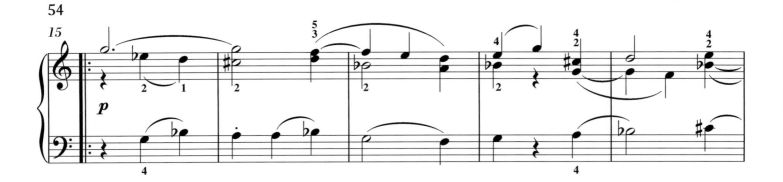

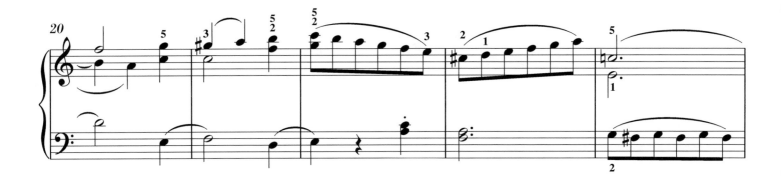

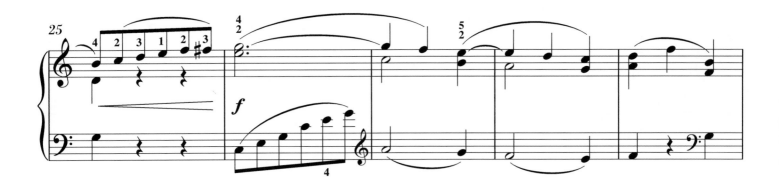

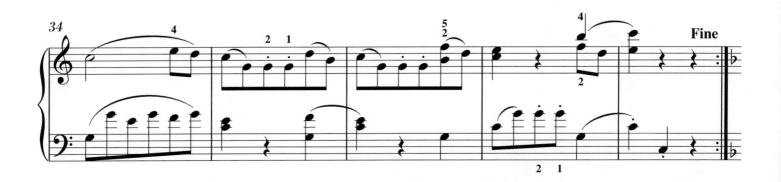

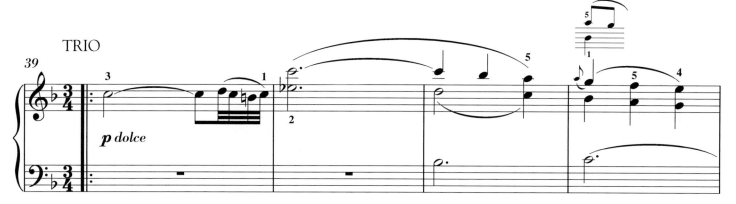

TRIO

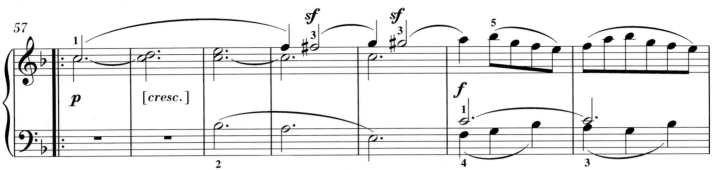

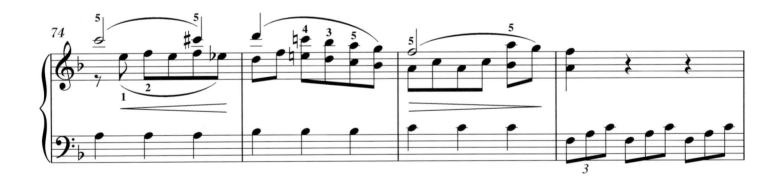

Menuetto da capo

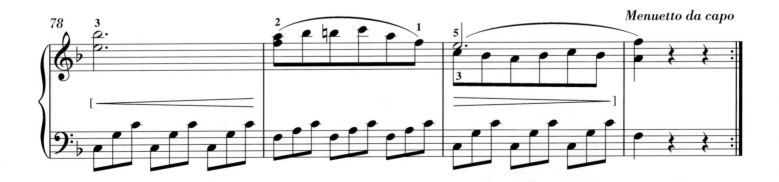

POLONAISE
[♩ = 80]

Sonatina No. 6 in C Major

Wolfgang Amadeus Mozart

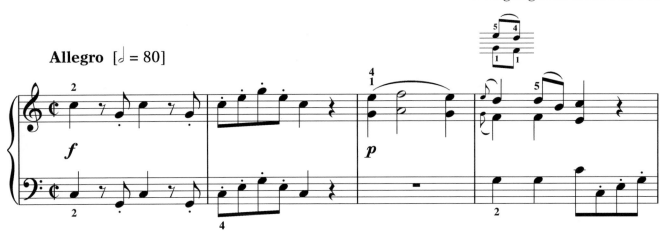

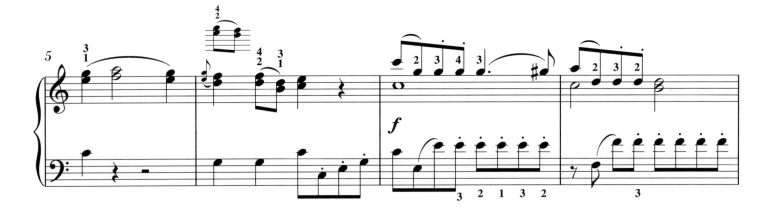

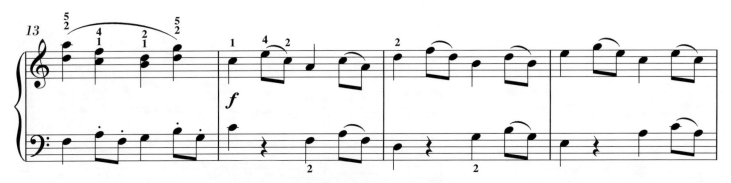

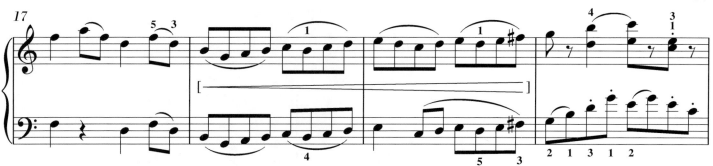

ossia

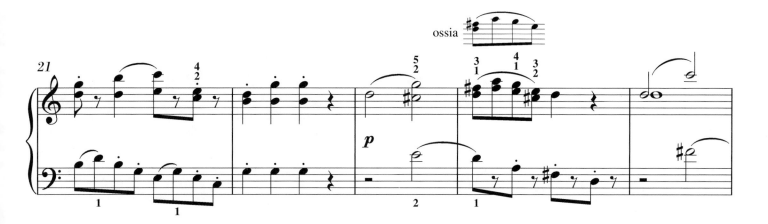

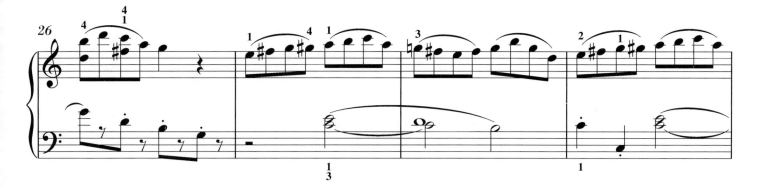

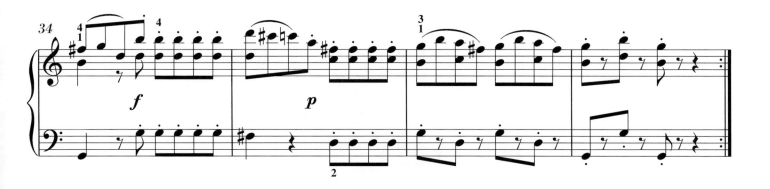

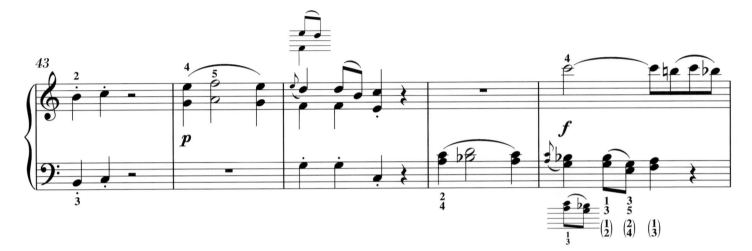

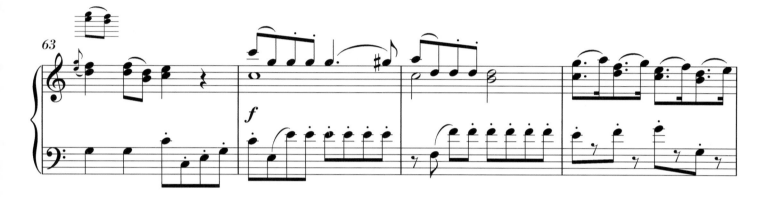

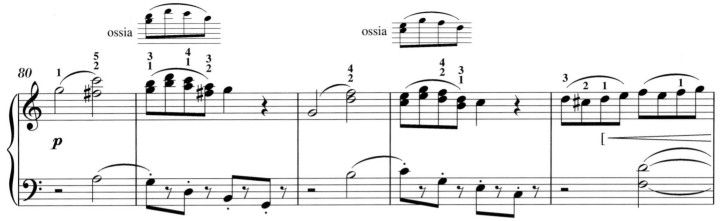

MENUETTO
Allegretto [♩ = 138]

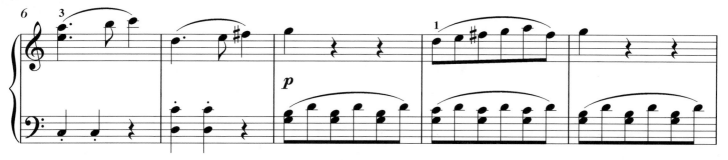

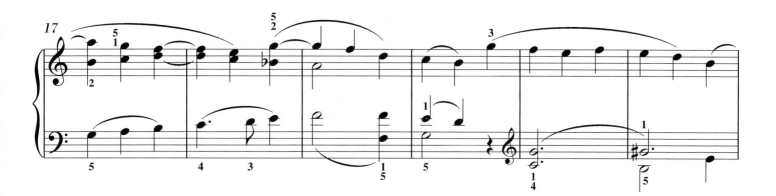

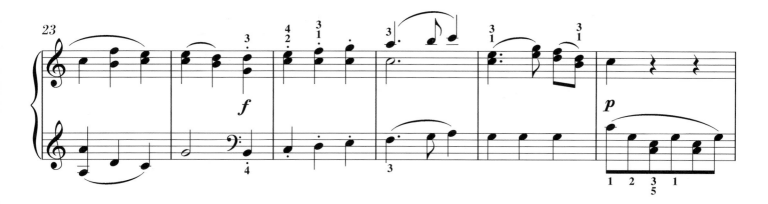

TRIO

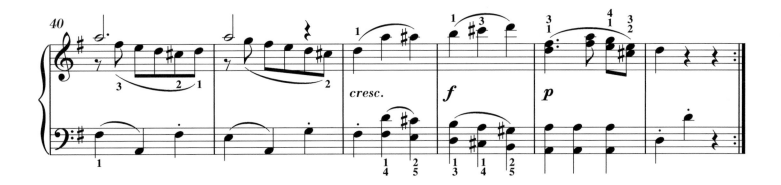

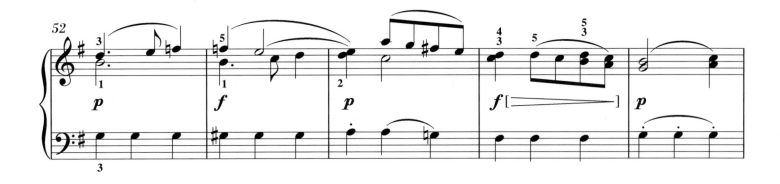

Adagio [♩ = 72]

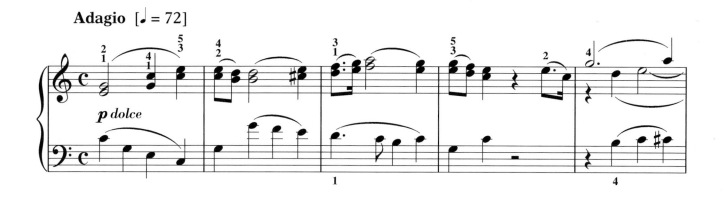

FINALE

Allegro [♩ = 158]

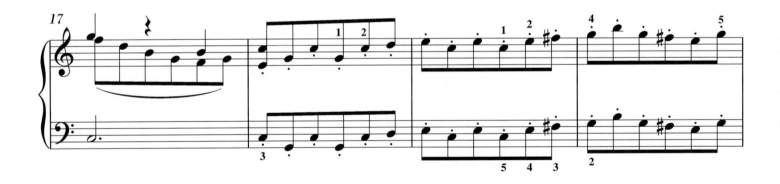

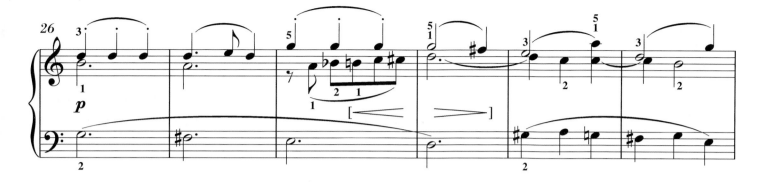

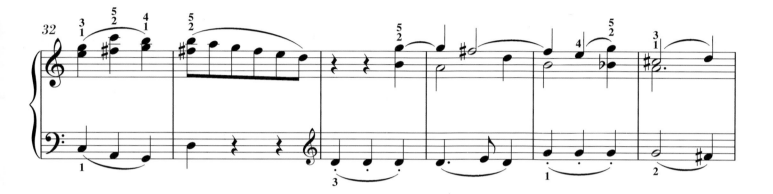

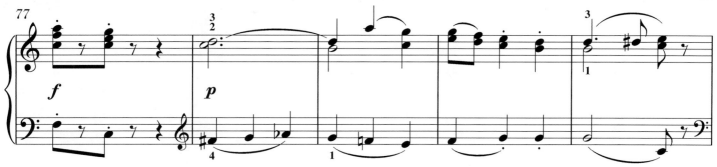

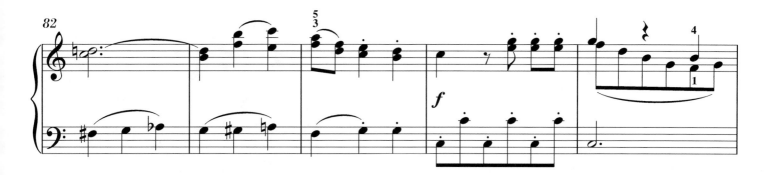

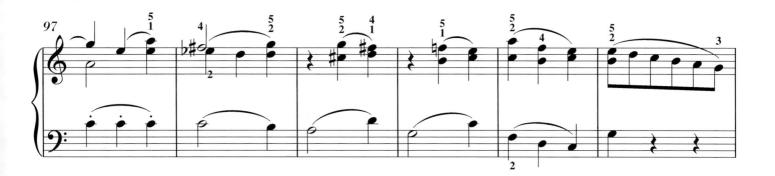

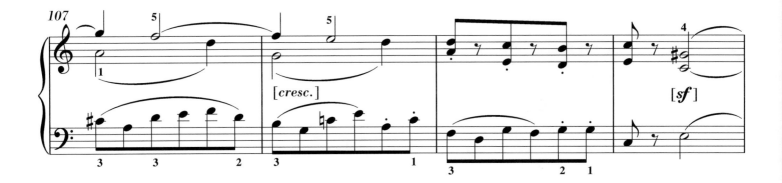

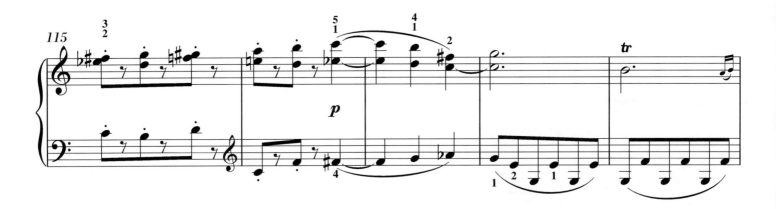

ABOUT THE EDITOR

CHRISTOPHER HARDING

Christopher Harding is on the artist faculty of the University of Michigan School of Music, Theatre and Dance. He has performed internationally and across the United States, generating enthusiasm and impressing audiences and critics alike with his substantive interpretations and pianistic mastery. He has given frequent solo, concerto and chamber music performances in venues as far flung as the Kennedy Center and Phillips Collection in Washington, D.C.; Suntory Hall in Tokyo and the National Theater Concert Hall in Taipei; the Jack Singer Concert Hall in Calgary, and halls and festival appearances in Newfoundland and Israel. His concerto performances have included concerts with the National Symphony and the Saint Louis Symphony Orchestras; the San Angelo and Santa Barbara Symphonies; and the Tokyo City Philharmonic, working with such conductors as Taijiro Iimori, Gisele Ben-Dor, Fabio Machetti, Randall Craig Fleisher, John DeMain, Ron Spiegelman, Daniel Alcott and Darryl One, among others. His chamber music and duo collaborations have included internationally renowned artists such as Karl Leister, András Adorján, and members of the St. Lawrence and Ying String Quartets, in addition to frequent projects with his distinguished faculty colleagues at the University of Michigan.

Professor Harding has presented master classes and lecture recitals at universities across the United States, Asia, Israel, and Canada. Additionally, he has extensively toured China under the auspices of the US State Department, and was in residence at the Sichuan Conservatory of Music as a Fulbright Senior Specialist at the invitation of the American Consulate in Chengdu, China.

Mr. Harding was born of American parents in Munich, Germany and raised in Northern Virginia. He holds degrees and Performer's Certificates from the Eastman School of Music and the Indiana University School of Music. His collegiate studies were with Menahem Pressler and Nelita True. Prior to college, he worked for ten years with Milton Kidd at the American University Department of Performing Arts Preparatory Division, where he was trained in the traditions of Tobias Matthay. He has taken twenty-five first prizes in national and international competitions, and in 1999 was awarded the special "Mozart Prize" at the Cleveland International Piano Competition, given for the best performance of a composition by Mozart.